I Can

Written by Leon Rosselson
Illustrated by Lorraine White

Collins Educational
An imprint of HarperCollins*Publishers*

I can tie my shoelace,

I can climb a tree,

I can run around the park.
You can't catch me!

I can paint a picture,

I can sing a song,

I can play with my friend
All day long.

I can play a whistle,
I can bang a drum,
I can make a tractor
With my mum.

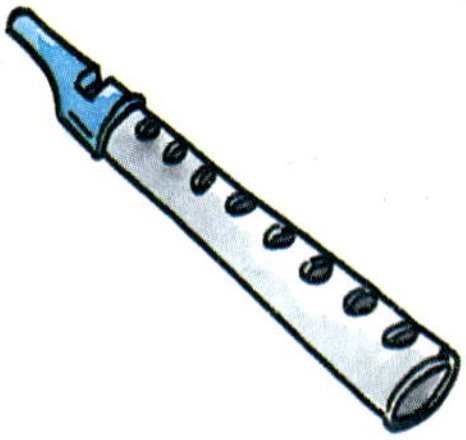

I can tie my shoelace,
I can climb a tree,
I can run around the park.
You can't catch me!

I can paint a picture,
I can sing a song,
I can play with my friend
All day long.